Helen
wishing you a
magical life

Wakefield

PERILUNE

by Mister Finch

Perilune
© 2019 Mister Finch

Photography and story by Mister Finch
Layout and design by Graham Pilling / Army of Cats Creative Studio

ISBN 978-1-5272-4543-3

First printing in the United Kingdom 2019.

www.mister-finch.com

Mister
Finch
TEXTILE ART

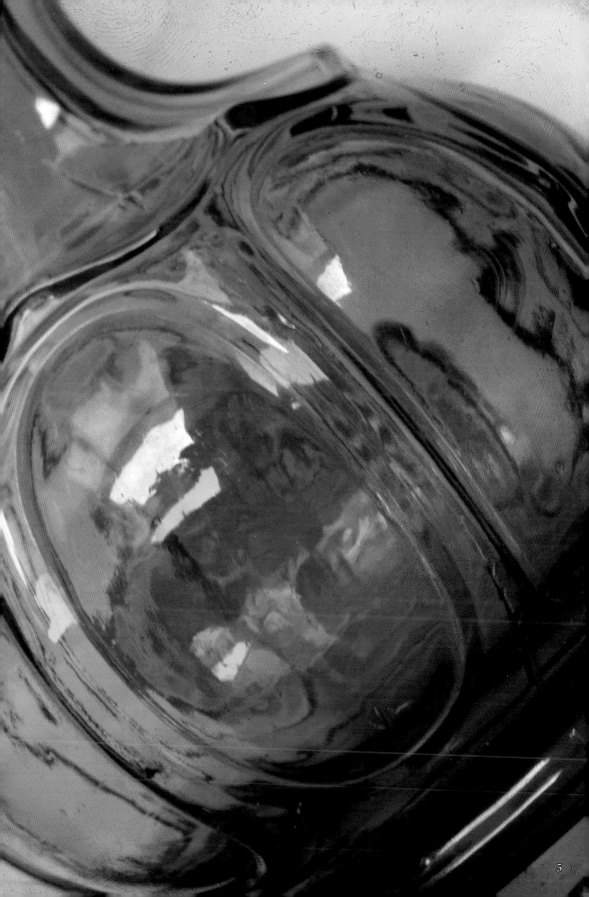

I wouldn't
be here
without the
moon's tears...

Houses.

They are all different, just like people.

Some you like, others... not so much.

The ones that you like just feel safe and warm
don't they?

You can walk in and feel right at home.

Sit down, kick off your shoes, and get comfy.

A place where you want to sit by the fire;

where the smell of baking wafts from the kitchen,

and where there's always

a fresh pot of tea being made.

That's love that you feel.

It's love that washes over the freshly made beds.

It's love that paints the walls and love that dusts the shelves.

Love that cooks the dinner,

hangs the shirts,

and bakes delicious smelling cakes.

Houses
that are loved
are a
wonderful
thing...

But
some houses
stop being loved.

The people leave for some reason
and don't ever come back...

The houses are left alone, abandoned and forgotten.
The beds are no longer made... the paint begins to peel...
and the curtains hang lifeless,
watching over the windows, sad and still.

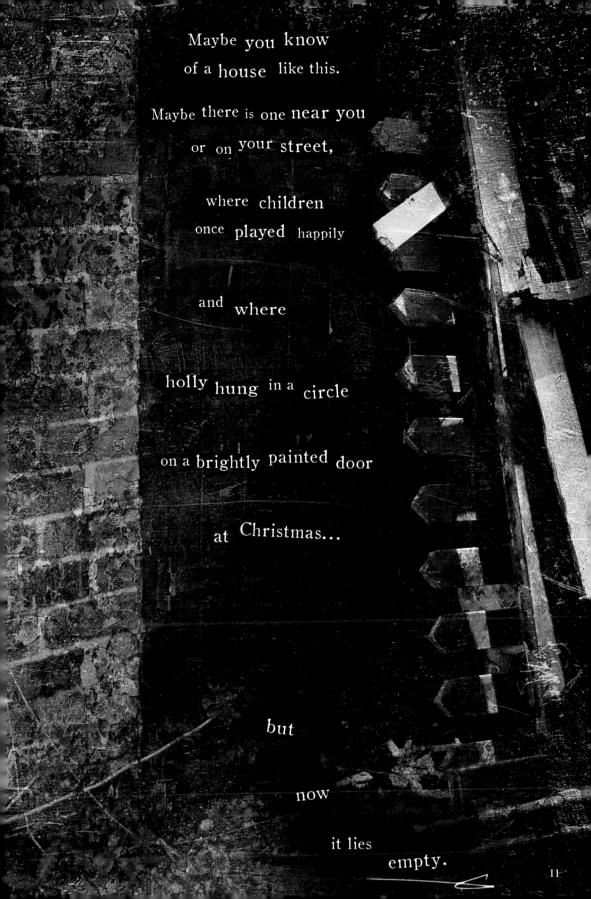

Maybe you know
of a house like this.

Maybe there is one near you
or on your street,

where children
once played happily

and where

holly hung in a circle

on a brightly painted door

at Christmas...

but

now

it lies
empty.

After all the years of holding the roof up strong,

hugging the windows tightly in place,

and breathing the doors in and out...

the sound of "happy birthday"

is replaced by the whistling wind.

The ticking clock heartbeat

is now one of dripping rain,

and windows

that were clean and bright

creak with broken shards

like the teeth

of a winter monster.

If the house could cry ...it would.

Slowly but surely

the love in the house

starts to become lonely...

it wants more love...

it *needs* more love.

Love always needs more love to cling to.

It misses the sound of laughter

and it misses people.

Quite terribly,

in fact.

The feeling of a nice house,   the *heart* of the house,

this is its spirit.

And it's born from love.

Magic folk call these house spirits 'marvelings'...

so this is what we shall call them

for they tend to know best.

A house never wants to fall apart...

it doesn't want to give up or give in...

It bangs its fists, it shouts out loud
and sometimes its spirit is strong enough
to do something quite remarkable.

It gathers up

pieces of **itself**

from its surroundings

foraging, searching,

scrambling, clawing...

for pieces of this
and
pieces of that.

A piece of a doorframe, perhaps,
some of the old curtains, maybe,
an old teacup... some bent wire...
building something

new and exciting,

strange
and
miraculous,

bizarre
and

extra ordinary...

something
wonderous...

The Marveling
begins to make itself its own new house,

its own special case,
its own
new home.

These
new houses

can be very complex.

Woven...
pulled...

stitched...
and
wired
together.

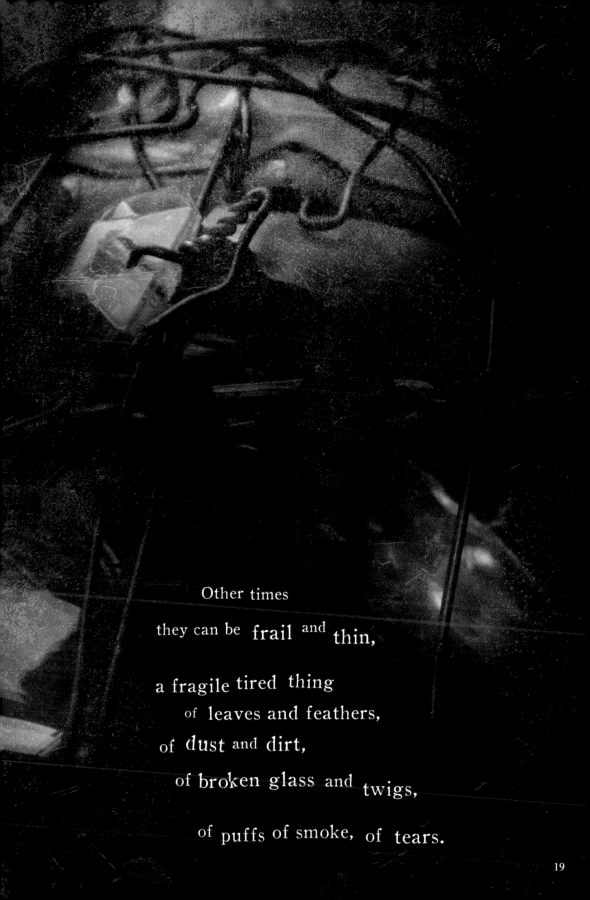

Other times

they can be frail and thin,

a fragile tired thing
of leaves and feathers,
of dust and dirt,
of broken glass and twigs,

of puffs of smoke, of tears.

Sometimes the house hasn't been
neglected or forgotten about...

If tragedy has befallen a house
there may be only fragments left...

The Marveling has to work fast
if it is to survive at all.

But surviving is what a
Marveling does best.

Marvelings - plate 2

23

Marvelings --- plate 3

Marvelings (plate 4)

Marvelings
Plate 6

27

MARVELINGS ~~~~~~~~~~~~~~ *plate 7*

Marveling (plate 9)

Marveling (plate 10)

Once the Marveling is inside its new house,

curled up and tucked in, its knees under its chin,

peeking out from its new dwelling...

it begins
to do something
unexpected

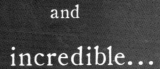

and

incredible...

it begins to

whistle.

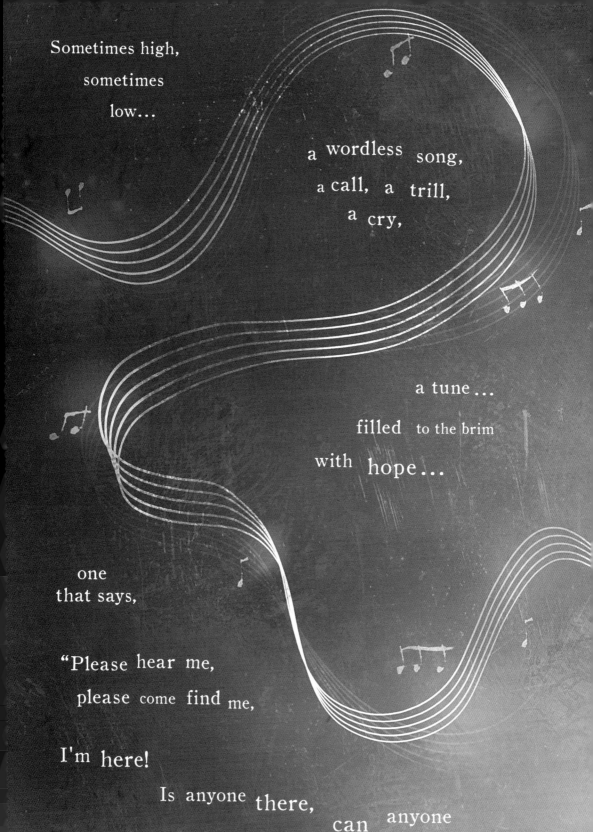

Sometimes high,
sometimes
low...

a wordless song,
a call, a trill,
a cry,

a tune...

filled to the brim

with hope...

one
that says,

"Please hear me,
please come find me,

I'm here!

Is anyone there,

can anyone

hear me?"

The whistle travels... an invisible ribbon
dancing through the air... swirling this way and that...
swimming up through leafy oak trees...

past the darkening wood
where the night owls meet.

It weaves through the rain
and skims over the
rivers and
streams...

it
floats
high over
the hedgerows
and chalky hills...

down through the garden gates,
past the neat flowerbeds
and the hanging washing...

and up and over the fields of whirling wheat,

down the cobbled lanes of the busy town...

until...

35

a set of ears begin to twitch...

long, beautiful, and made of fur...

ears that belong to...

Perilune.

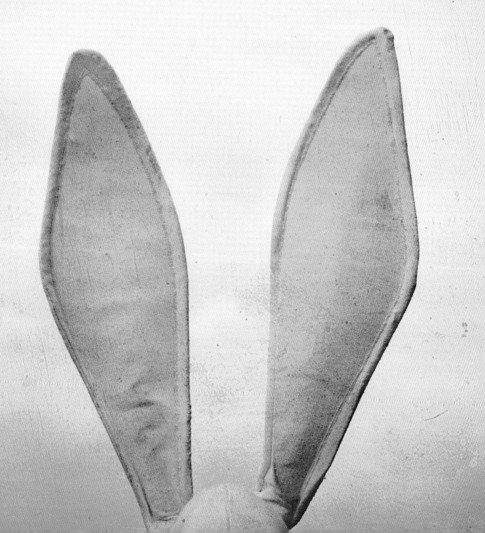

His **coat** is a
midnight sky
filled with
stars.

His shoes
are made from
seaweed
leather...

and have been kissed
by a thousand fishes.

He knows old Magic...

...and

Secret

Ways...

...and works by candlelight
deep within the Grotto-Burrow.

When he has

the time...

He enjoys the odd game
and a bit of company...

He loves the bees
and always does what he can
to protect them.

He loves to play

his Moon Guitar...

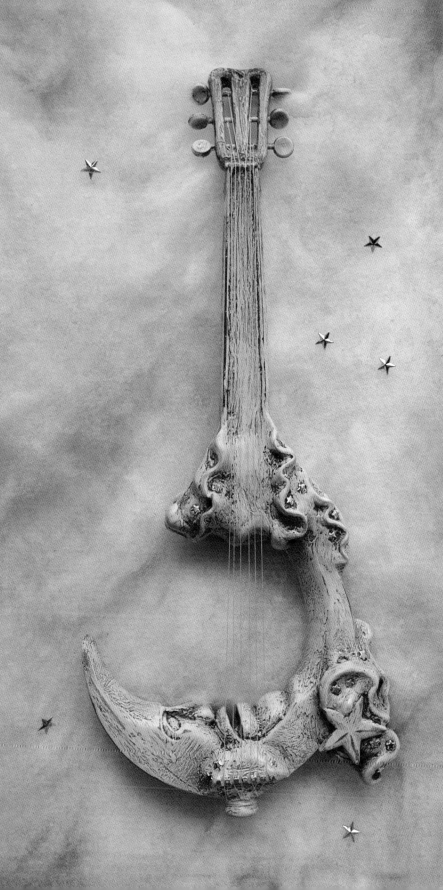

and

on

windy

days

he

flies

his

kite.

But not today...

today, he must pack
his trusty case

for there are
whistles in the air...

"I'm coming,
my darling!"

he says,

"I can
hear you!"

Once his cart is fully packed
with all the things he'll need,
Perilune's journey begins...

It's always a pleasure to bump into the Hooty Owl children...

"I've **found** you!"

he says

as the Marveling whistles

with excitement

and

relief.

With great care
Perilune scoops up
the nervous little
Marveling...

and
places it
gently
in his
cart.

some days there are many
whistles to listen for

and
many more
Marvelings to find.

A sign catches
Perilune's
eye...

Cocktail
Bar →

and reminds him
of something
long ago…

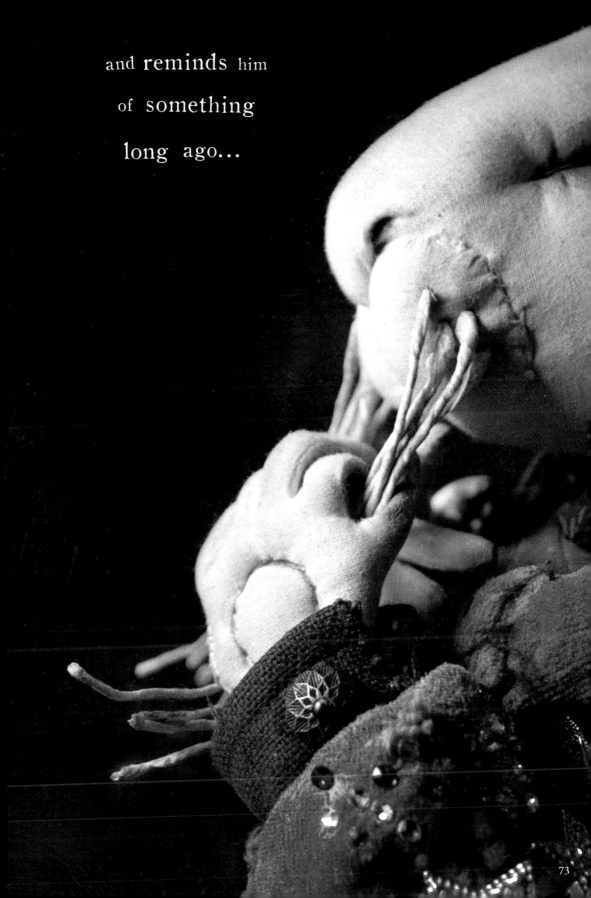

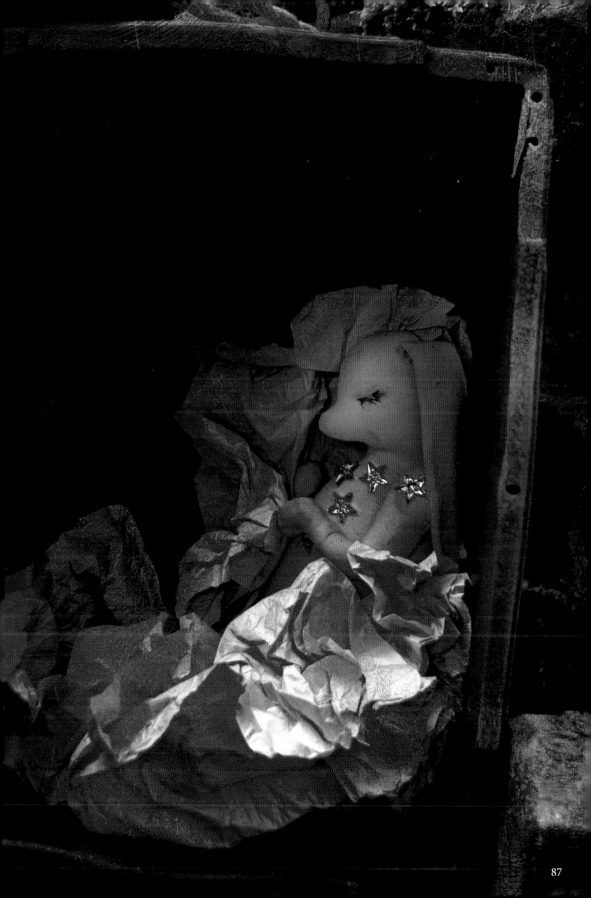

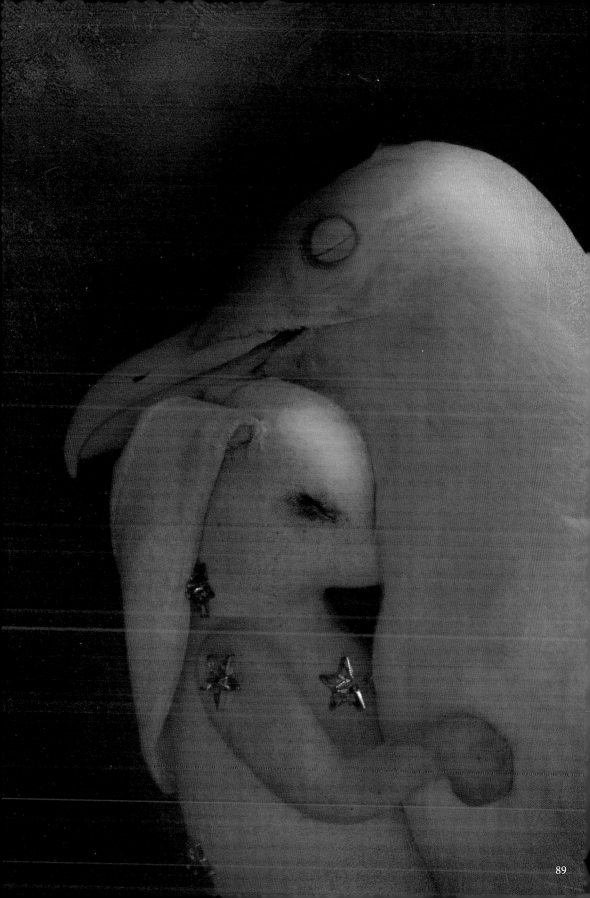

Cocktail Bar →

"But what
happens now?"
I hear you ask,

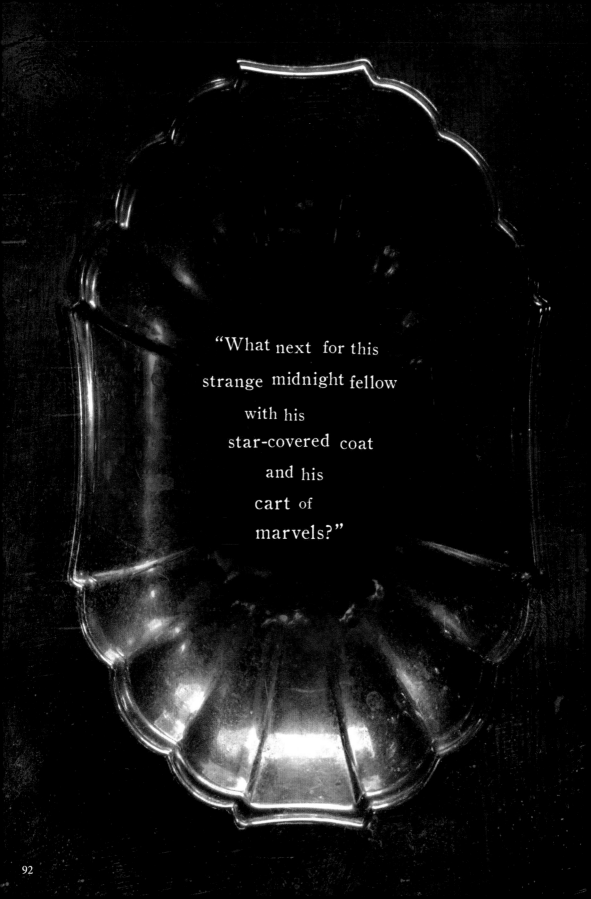

"What next for this
strange midnight fellow
with his
star-covered coat
and his
cart of
marvels?"

Perilune and his whistling cargo must travel onwards...

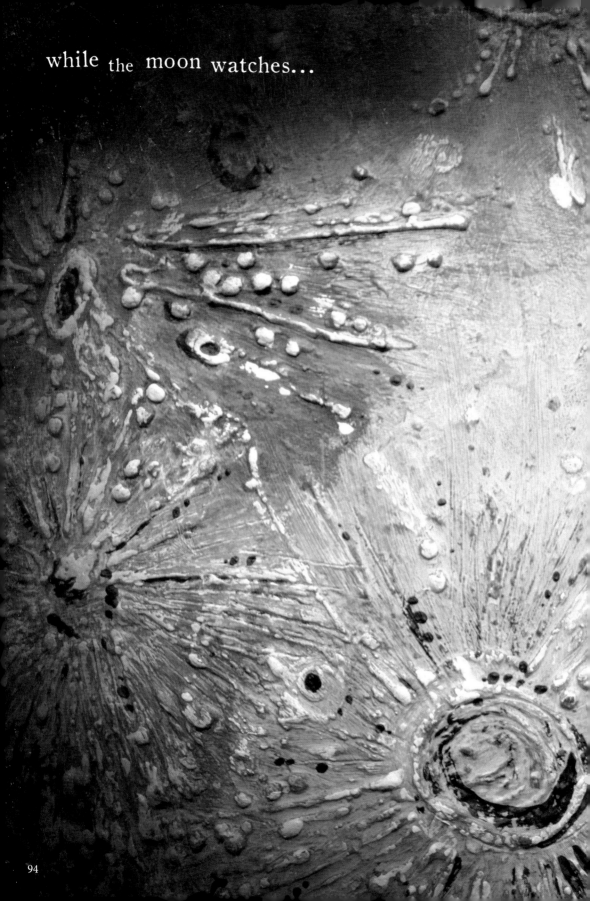

while the moon watches...

and sees

everything...

The stars
are his guide

when the days have
ripened into shadows.

He braves

the snow...

the
rain...

and the
biting cold...

all the way
to the beach
    and
onwards...

to the wide open sea.

As the sun goes down, Perilune swirls his silver staff,

making patterns and shapes in the sand.

And then he begins to sing...

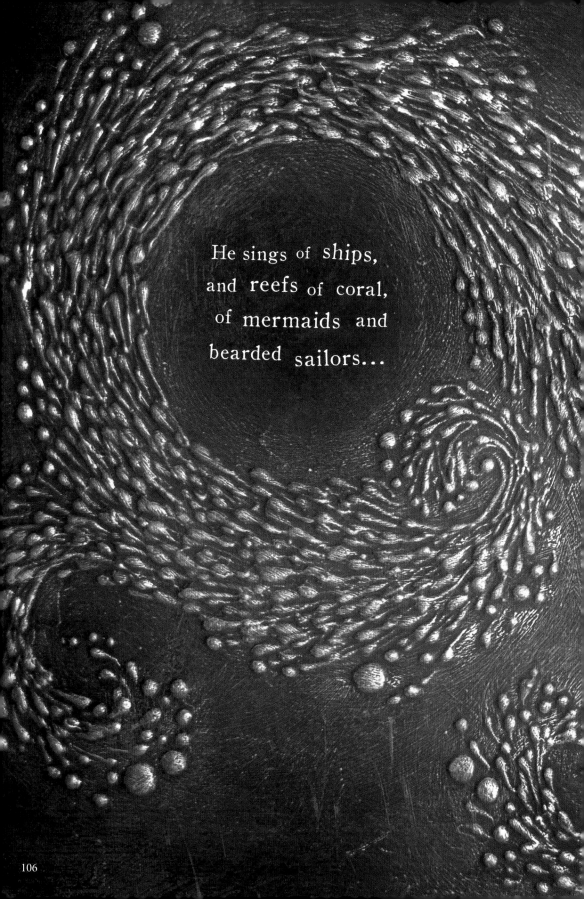

He sings of ships,
and reefs of coral,
of mermaids and
bearded sailors...

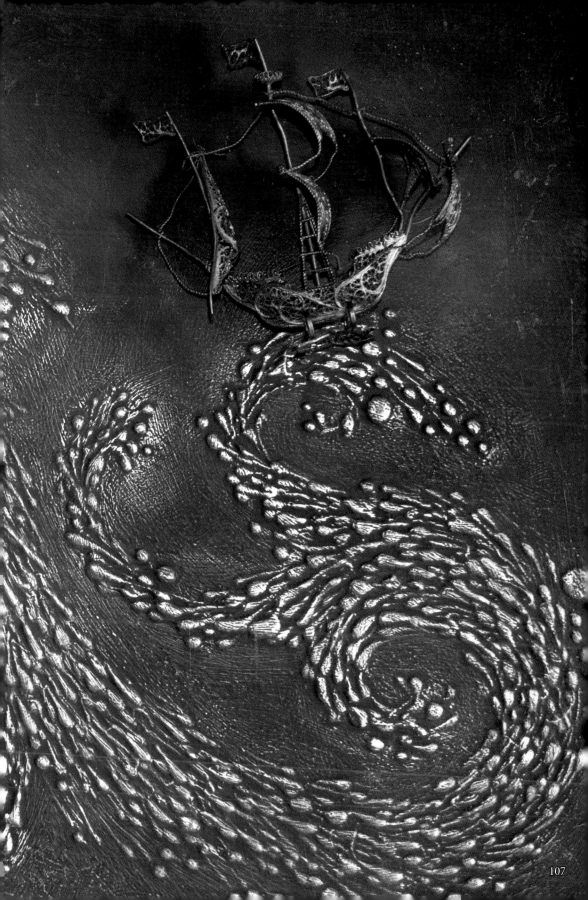

of white horses...

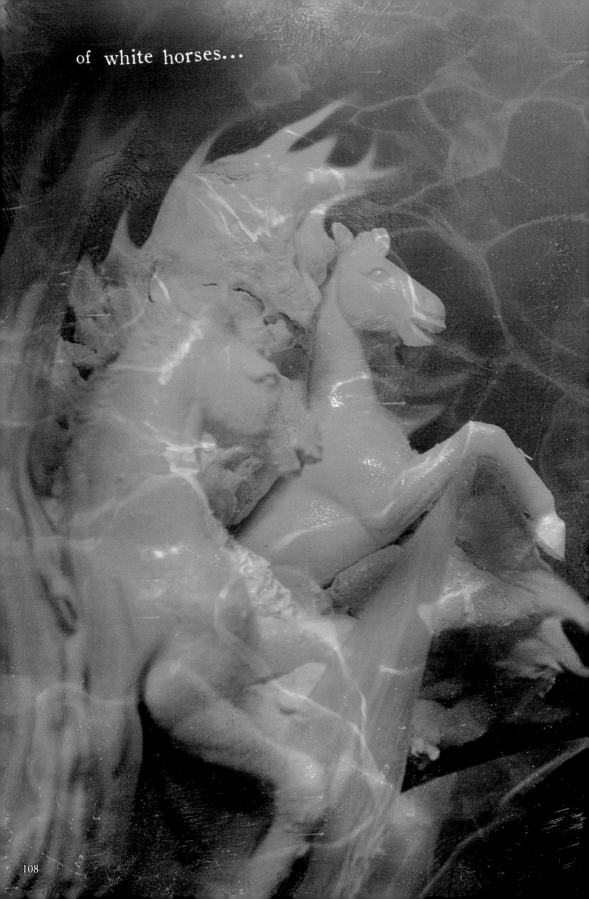

barnacle-covered

whales

and fish who light up the inky depths

with secret spectrums and firefly eyes.

Turning now to his
trusty cart

he gently
lifts out a
Marveling...

and then s l o w l y...

c a r e f u l l y...

opens it.

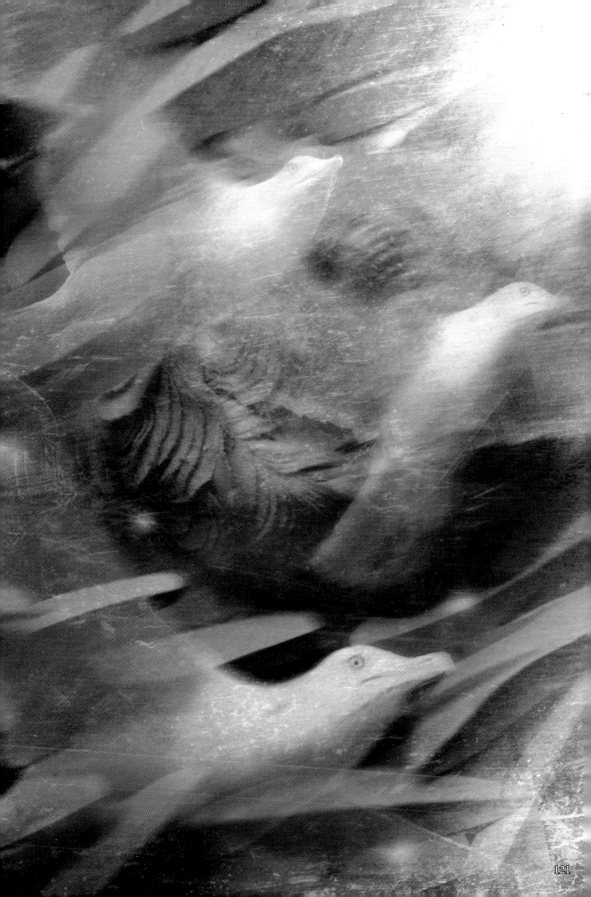

"Be free! Fly!"

shouts Perilune

as the air fills with circling

and swooping seabirds.

Under the light of the moon, the sea spell has

transformed the Marveling.

Perilune opens
the remaining Marvelings,
one by one,

and releases them into the air.

No longer lonely or forgotten,

these little spirits are now free

to roam the land, and sea and sky,

wherever the wind blows.

So the next time

you see a seagull

swooping overhead...

Pay close attention...

it might just be

a Marveling.

The
End

Acknowledgements:

This book is for Dildy the Darly Beau.

Big thanks to all my family and friends. Extra big thanks go to Graham Pilling from Army of Cats for all his help in bringing my images to life and working so hard with layouts and grammar and so much more.

A thank you must also go out to the Caddisfly larvae for giving me the idea with their incredible protective cases.

Mister Finch   *July 2019*